Do Pets And Other Animals Go To Heaven?

How To Recover From The Loss Of An Animal Friend

Cheryl Renee' Webb

BriteBooks
www.BriteBooks.org

Published By:
BriteBooks
P.O. Box 801
Ortonville, MI 48462-0801
U.S.A.

E-mail: info@BriteBooks.org
Website: www.BriteBooks.org

Edited by: Susan Frazier
Printed in the USA

Library of Congress Cataloging-in-Publication Data
Webb, Cheryl R.
Do Pets And Other Animals Go To Heaven?
How To Recover From The Loss Of An Animal Friend
LCCN 2002096004

ISBN 0-9726363-0-7

Table of Contents

About The Author

Cheryl Renee' Webb has been married to her husband Tom for over 32 years. She is the mother of two. A daughter Renee' and a son Tom and she is a soon to be grandmother. Cheryl moved from Illinois to Michigan in 1978 when her husband was transferred. They bought a small farm in southern Michigan where she raised her family along with a myriad of pets and farm animals.

Cheryl has been teaching and counseling from the Bible for over 22 years helping and comforting many people and their families. She is active in her local church as well as teaching and ministering in a local retirement village for the past 14 years.

Currently her home is situated where deer, beaver, ducks, pheasant and a whole host of wildlife have their home. You can contact her by E-mail at: crwebb@britebooks.org or by writing to: BriteBooks Dept. 11, P.O. Box 801, Ortonville, MI 48462-0801

FOREWORD

By: Author's Husband

I vividly remember the day this book was born. It was on a cold, rainy Mother's Day when our cat Sooty died. I can still see myself standing on the north side of the house digging a grave under the apple tree. There was still a thin layer of frost in the ground from a long and hard winter. In the middle of digging I turned around and looked through the hallway window into the house. I saw my two children standing on either side of Cheryl with tears rolling down their faces and tissues in their hands.

Renee', the oldest, was about six years old. She had somewhat more understanding about death than Tommy who was just two. She was visibly shaken and upset. My heart was broken too, but not so much by the death of Sooty as by the sorrow in my children and wife. It was Mother's Day. What a cruel joke for death to play on a day that was to be happy and joyous.

I turned away and went back to the job of digging, mainly to hide the tears that were starting to roll down my own face. I spoke out loud to myself and told death, "Some day you'll no longer have any power over us or our pets." I look forward to that day with joy. But what was I going to do now? How will we comfort our children? How can we salvage such a gloomy Mother's Day?

On that day this book was born in the heart and mind of Cheryl. Out of that gloomy, grief - filled Mother's Day has come a blessing to our family and now to yours. As you read the pages of this book and make these truths and ideas your own, you will be able to comfort yourself as well as others when the time arises. In addition to comfort you will receive hope for the future and learn how you can live with your pets forever.

ACKNOWLEDGMENTS

I wish heartfelt thanks to Rebecca Springer, Betty Malz, Roberts Lairdon and Jesse Duplantis for sharing their revelations, insights and personal experiences of Heaven. Without their message of "the place prepared for us in Heaven" this book would have been difficult to write.

I could not have written this book if I had not been taught about God's unlimited and unchanging love for us all. Therefore I want to thank my Pastors of 17 years, Rev. Bill and Jean Tulip. They taught me by their words as well as by their demonstration of love. I thank God for the blessing they have been to me and my family.

I'd also wish to thank my husband Tom, my wonderful daughter Renee', my son Tom and his wife Nichole. They all encouraged me and dared to call me an author. Without them there would be no "Do Pets and Other Animals Go To Heaven?"

How To Use This Book

This book has been divided into six sections to enable the reader to find specific topics quickly and easily. Basically each section can be read on its own without having to read the previous section first. Even though I have written it this way, I encourage everyone to read the whole book to gain a deeper understanding and to build a greater foundation upon which to stand when facing grief from loss.

The death of a pet or animal friend is traumatic. This book offers more than preserving memories of the past. It is my sincerest desire for all that read through these pages to obtain comfort, hope and peace. The purpose is to help build a vision of your pet or animal friend in Heaven. This vision can be deposited in your heart where you can reflect on it at any time. There are enough difficult struggles to get through in one lifetime without adding the stressful mourning over the loss of an animal. I believe you will be encouraged and comforted through reading this book.

I have included some photos of the pets *(some of which are in Heaven now)* and family members mentioned in this book. I hope you enjoy them.

It is my sincerest desire that "Do Pets and Other Animals Go To Heaven?" bring you great Peace, Comfort and Joy.

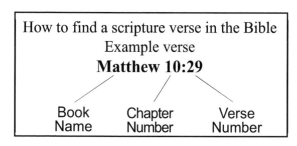

I'm practicing to be a mom with a "not so happy" Cat. -- Porky

Our first apartment... Only one bathroom so I have to wait my turn. -- Beaver & Porky

SECTION ONE

THE QUEST FOR ANSWERS

WHERE DID SOOTY GO?

Pets are an enjoyable and often a necessary part of life. We love them, train them, show them off, brag on them, and tell wild and wonderful stories about them. They are so dear to our hearts, dearer than some people.

Then, one cruel day they're gone, leaving a void in our lives. We yearn for and miss the companionship and unconditional love they gave. If only we could see them again. Is there life after death for our pets? What happens to their soul? Do our pets and other animals go to Heaven?

Questions. Questions. What are the answers? Where can I find comfort and hope for the pain I am feeling? Is there a solid foundation on which to build peace and hope?

When pets of mine have died, I always thought their soul or spirit went into a nebulous somewhere leaving me alone, in pain with only a memory. I had no hope that I would ever see my pets again.

I was seven when my dad brought home a beautiful collie puppy we named Buddy. He was a wonderful friend who had an innate ability to console and understand a little girl. He was the only pet I ever had growing up and was terribly missed when he was 'put to sleep'. I had all sorts of emotions and thoughts bottled inside because Buddy had been my best friend. No one told me he was going to be put down, I didn't realize he suffered from severe arthritis; no one bothered to help me through a very sad time. Where was my friendly black, white and tan collie? He was just gone.

Looking for some consolation, I told my friend across the street what had happened; she was unsympathetic. She treated my sorrow with little concern; she wanted to talk about her vacation. I was left with my own ideas and imaginations. For some reason my parents never thought to talk with me and help heal the black hole in my heart. I cried, but never let anyone see me. I hid and closed off that chapter of life in my heart for many years to come.

When my husband Tom and I married we lived in a little apartment in the crowded suburbs of Chicago. We often talked about getting a pet but, decided it was unfair to any animal to live in such cramped quarters in a busy town. We felt pets needed a yard and no busy traffic close by.

Two years later we moved into a town house and through friendly persuasion inherited a dog. We soon gave her away. The yard space was very limited and no fences were allowed. Coupled with that was too many children and busy traffic to contend with. It wasn't until Tom's employer transferred him to Michigan that pets became a real possibility for us.

We moved into our 100 year old farm house on 10 acres with 2 large barns just three days before Thanksgiving 1978. Our two little children and two small cats loved the farm. Our new home town was tiny with limited traffic. We lived 5 miles north of it with acres of room for pets. It was cold that day with snow swirling as we huddled together in front of the fireplace to keep warm. With all our city smarts we had one heck of a time trying to start a fire in the ancient coal furnace. Not until after putting our children to bed in snow suits and knit caps did it dawn on us that in moving here we had also moved back in time to the brink of pioneer living. That Thanksgiving was truly memorable and topped off when another cat, who had apparently made her home in our barn, showed up at the back door ready for some turkey leftovers.

After learning to start and keep fires going all day and all night, our next family project was to pick a suitable dog. As long as I could remember I'd always wanted a large dog so that's what we got. She was a beautiful Golden Lab/St. Bernard puppy whom we named Winter Noel. It was thrilling for us to have a dog. It made our family feel complete. The only thing left to do was figure out how to keep everyone warm during the coming winter.

When spring came, Winter Noel's true inbred nature was revealed. She enthusiastically ate the twelve chickens I raised from chicks, feathers and all. In addition to the chickens were numerous pieces of furniture, the frozen meat set out to defrost for dinner and the Christmas Tree. We lost count of the number of screen doors Tom replaced because she just wouldn't wait for us to open the door when she wanted out.

Somewhere we had failed as dog raisers. We gave Winter (whom we renamed Wiener) away to the unsuspecting dog pound that wanted to train her as a guide dog for the blind. What a hoot!

A few months after Winter left for greener pastures we bumped into an opportunity to inherit another dog. I had had my fill of dogs. Any desire for another dog had jumped through the last newly repaired screen door with Winter Noel. I was not having any more dogs… but the children… their sad eyes and pleading lips, I succumbed to the pressure. We were now the proud owners of a two-year-old pedigree Sheltie named Jessie. I am happy to say she was a much better family dog.

By mid spring, our barn cat and dog were propagating faster than we could count. Puppies were being birthed in the barn while kittens were climbing the curtains, hiding under the sofa and crawling down the heating vent in the parlor. It seemed every few months we were standing in front of the Kroger, our local grocery store trying to give away pet offspring. This experience made us firm believers in having our non-pedigree pets spayed or neutered

One of the male cats brought from Chicago belonged to me and the other to my daughter Renee'. It was a cold Mother's Day when my favorite cat Sooty, a Siamese mix, died in my arms. He was as black as the coal we shoveled into our furnace. He always sat on my lap and slept by my pillow. We had a bonding I hadn't permitted myself to have since my dog Buddy had died. Once again I was confronted with the death of a beloved pet. The whole ordeal was devastating.

My children and I cried and watched from the hall window as Tom buried him under the apple tree north of the house. My heart was broken, again. I never wanted to be attached to another pet as long as I lived. What happened to him? Where did he go? Was he in Heaven? How does God feel about animals? What answers of comfort could I give my children? Would the pain from this loss ever go away?

Sooty's death was the driving force that sent me on the quest to find the answers to these questions. I never dreamed I would find so many answers or experience such great comfort and hope. I truly hope that what I've discovered will help you as much as it has helped me.

Porky pretends to be a new baby for me until Renee' arrives.

My childhood collie Buddy posing with the boy next door.

My husband's boyhood pets... Charlie, Cookie & Cleo. Cookie in the middle was the puppy of Cleo. Looks like it must have been nap time..

Renee' and Cookie share an ice cream cone.

Freckles gets a great big hug from baby Renee'

SECTION TWO

BUILDING A FIRM FOUNDATION

STARTING POINT

There is one thing people differing in creeds, beliefs, nations, tongues, and tribes have in common. Pets. People everywhere have pets. From Africa to Asia to the Americas pets fulfill a very real need in peoples lives.

It is the death of our pets I wanted to know more about. I asked, "What happened to Sooty when he died?" I never received an answer I could obtain comfort with. Most of the time I was told "I don't know". That was no good, I needed concrete answers. I wanted solutions I could stand on without having constant doubts.

To understand where my pets went when they died, I had to find out where they came from. Now, I'm not ignorant of the birds and bees, so obviously I'm not speaking reproductively. It stands to reason at some point, in the mother's womb life entered. It seemed logical that if I could learn the source of that life I would find the answers about my pet's death.

The only source of life I could think of was to be found in the Bible. I methodically searched out Bible verses the same as an archeologist uses a fine pointed trowel and small brush to uncover truths about a past civilization. I let these verses build a foundation as I uncovered truths about, "What happens to our pets and other animals when they die?"

The scriptures were taken from the King James Version of the Bible. I took the liberty to eliminate thee's and thou's and used our everyday language for easier understanding. All the references are included so that you can take your own Bible and find them. For example, Psalm 104:1 would be found in the book of Psalms, chapter 104, verse 1.

As I searched for truth I found it. I gained the comfort I so badly needed. It was amazing how a book, written about and for people, is filled with verse about animals. There are more than 3,000 verses that deal with animals and God's relationship with them.

I have no desire or ambition to be religious or dogmatic. This is not a theological dissertation. It is about animals and pets, yours and mine. So, even if you have never read the Bible, take a look at what I've uncovered and judge for yourself

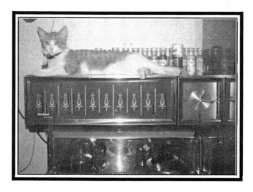

Beaver waits for dinner on a nice warm stove.

IN THE BEGINNING

A good place to start is the beginning. I opened to the book of Genesis (beginnings) where God is about to replenish the Earth. On the fifth day sea creatures, large and small and flying creatures great and small, were created. On the sixth day every sort of cattle, creature, beast, and creeping thing was created. The plan was for the animals to be fruitful and multiply in the seas and on the earth. God saw that this was GOOD! In God's opinion animals are good. Genesis 1:21, 25 & 31.

After creating the animals, God created man, male and female. God gave the male and female specific instructions to live in the world He made for them. These instructions included having dominion over and caring for the earth and the animals.

Genesis 9:2 states, every beast of the earth, every fowl of the air, all that move upon the earth, and all the fishes of the sea have been delivered into our hands. We are to be in dominion over them as well as provide care for them.

At a recent dog show I noticed people exercising this dominion. With a verbal command or hand gesture the animal would perform excellence in obedience. Many were performing tricks and showing off their fine pedigree. My father trained and showed my childhood dog Buddy. I helped my dad in the training and watched and cheered when Buddy won medals and awards in competitions. Just like Buddy, every dog had a name. They slept in special beds, and stood on grooming tables loaded with brushes, combs, ribbons and bows.

Just like when I was young, owners still spend hours brushing, grooming, patting, braiding, attaching hats and fancy collars to their beloved pet. Who would go through all that trouble for a creature that lacked importance? The owners' pride and enjoyment greatly overshadowed the work involved in preening their 'Fido'.

After God created the animals He wanted them to have names, so Adam got the job. God desires animals to have names. Who gives a name to anything that has no importance? Names denote individuality, like Sooty who was black as the coal we shoveled into our old furnace. Most people name their pets based on their personality, appearance, and so on. God, just like us, wanted animals to have names.

Call someone a pig, then ask him or her "Does that offend you?" If they don't hit you first, you'll probably get an answer. "Pig" denotes specific personality, appearance, social grace or habits. To give an animal a name was God's idea first. Today we bring that desire into everyday life.

USING OUR DOMINION

Using God given dominion over animals is more challenging than naming pets. I was very surprised when I began my research for I never knew I had dominion, let alone how to use it. There were many animals I was afraid of, such as stray dogs and horses. I wanted to turn the tables and operate in the position of dominion and authority God had given people. As I studied I began to understand the God given position of authority and dominion on the earth. It was a different way of thinking with me being in dominion rather than the animal. I stumbled around for a while in this somewhat unfamiliar territory, but the more I used my dominion, the greater success I had.

After the Sheltie, Jessie, came to live with us she displayed negative habits learned as a puppy. Unknown to us at first, she had been an abused pet by her original owner. For instance, when I called her, if I didn't use just the right tone of voice, she would not come. It was frustrating to have to run outside and corral the dog into the house. The angrier I got, the more she ran from me. Ten acres are a lot of ground to cover.

Finally, I realized she was not going to change. I was the one who must change. So, I did. I began using my dominion in a different way. I stopped threatening her and stopped calling her "bad dog". I began telling her she was "good girl". Even when she ran into the fields, I called after her "Good girl!" Gradually, she changed. The change in me produced a change in her. I realized that God's interest in the well being and care of animals was greater than mine was because, after all, it was his plan of dominion that brought such wonderful change in Jessie and me. Dominion in love had been his solution all the time.

What I had learned prepared me to use my authority and dominion whenever I had to. One day it came unexpectedly while riding my bike down a country road. Up in front of me stood a dog. As I made eye contact with him I knew, by the look in his eye, I was going to be his next meal. But, amazingly, something greater than fear rose up inside, a new principle came to mind: the principle of dominion and authority. Suddenly confidence arose. As he RAN close to the bike and tried to attack me, I immediately took dominion over that dog. I yelled "sit" and he did. Three times I told it to "sit". He did! Every time I spoke, the dog stopped and sat down. Ha! I was impressed!

Finally, I was so far ahead the dog gave up and went away. The dominion we have works. It is not to abuse but to protect our pets and us. That dog's nose in a bicycle chain or spokes would have ruined his day, not to mention mine. I didn't get bit, but my heart sure got a workout!

ANIMALS ARE PART OF GOD'S RICHES

Psalm 104:24-25 states, God made every type of animal with wisdom; the earth is full of HIS RICHES. Wisdom is the ability to apply knowledge. The thought and effort involved in creating such a great variety of animal life on the earth is nothing short of monumental. Wisdom, understanding and knowledge all had a part in the creation. I believe God had an enjoyable time thinking up all the different animals? When they were created he surely had us in mind. He made them as a source of pleasure and enjoyment for us as well as for himself.

When I ask people what riches are to them, their first answer is usually money. Jewels, gold, silver, cars, houses, and real estate are some things that follow. Psalm 104:24-25 mentions God's riches. Those riches refer to ANIMAL LIFE: so great and wide a sea where in things creeping innumerable both great and small, dwell, in the sea, in the air and on dry land. Animals are God's riches.

These riches of God's, all animals, but especially our pets, are for us to enjoy. God gives us richly all things to enjoy (1Timothy 6:17). This truth points out to me that if animals give us enjoyment here then we can expect enjoyment with them in Heaven. I think it is safe to say Heaven is a better place. If we enjoy our pets and animals here, how much more can we expect to enjoy them in Heaven?

GOD'S PROMISES TO ANIMALS

Have you ever promised your pet a treat or a ride in the car? Have you ever reneged or forgotten that promise? I have. Pets don't remember if promises are broken do they? Yet, God treats animals as though they do. How important are promises to animals?

I came to the account in the Bible about the flood in Noah's day. It was God's idea to save every species of animal so that they would again populate the earth. He had Noah follow intricate plans to build a sailing vessel that would hold every species of animal. The ark was so large it took Noah and his sons over 100 years to build it. Genesis 6:14-22.

After forty days and nights of rain, it was several more months before Noah could open the door of the ark and let out the animals, himself and his family. When the land was sufficiently dry, Noah opened the door and the animals went out to replenish the earth.

God made a promise and sealed it with a sign as a remembrance. Maybe you've seen the sign of His promise lately, it's the rainbow. He promised there would never be another flood to cover the entire earth. Noah received this promise, but not him alone. The animals received the promise also. God wanted the animals to be just as reassured as Noah. God made and kept his promise to the animals because they are important to Him as well as to us. Genesis 9:8-17.

Does God care about animals? The answer is yes! Does God care about our pets? Yes, assuredly, yes! He made a promise to the animals and has been keeping it for thousands of years. God cares about our pets; they are important to Him.

In the book of Jonah the animals join with the people of Nineveh in changing their mind and changing their direction of life-styles. (Chapter 3, verses 6-8). The animals along with the people fasted and covered themselves with ashes and sackcloth. At the end of the story, Jonah was upset because a gourd died. God was astounded since he wanted to save the whole city of Nineveh plus all beasts. As I thought about this I realized that without any livestock left alive, in that time frame, that city of upwards of 620,000 people would have been in serious trouble. It is no surprise that the livestock was included in the repentance. God truly cares about people and animals.

Our pets are important to God, yet, people are more important. Our happiness, joy, and peace are priorities to God right here and now. Our pets give us much enjoyment, companionship and comfort. Why would our pets no longer be important to God after they die? *What is important to us is important to God. The pets that bring us happiness here are important to God.* Ephesians 2:7 states: That in the ages to come he might show the exceeding riches of his grace in kindness toward us through Christ Jesus. That exceeding kindness includes our pets being in Heaven if for no other reason than just to make us happy.

ANIMAL ABUSE - WHAT DOES GOD THINK OF IT?

There is a lot of welcomed talk these days about stopping animal abuse. PETA, and other humane societies such as the ASPCA, Anti-Cruelty Society and Doris Day Animal League save many animals from cruel exploitation. Senseless poaching, inhumane trapping and medical experimentation is not a new problem. The following story from the Old Testament reveals God's heart on animal abuse. (Numbers 22:1-33)

The king of Moab was at war with Israel, and he wanted to win. In order to be assured of a victory he believed a curse must be established against Israel. The king of Moab hired a greedy prophet, named Balaam to pronounce that curse. The king promised Balaam money and gifts if he would accomplish the King's wishes.

Balaam saddled his donkey and rode from Moab to Israel. As he approached Israel, the donkey he rode stopped dead in her tracks. She saw, standing in front of her, the Angel of the Lord with his sword of fire drawn. The donkey turned abruptly, and went into the field on Balaam's left. Balaam, who didn't see the angel, hit the donkey with his staff to turn her back onto the road.

When the donkey saw the Angel of the Lord again, she thrust herself into the wall on the right of the path, crushing Balaam's foot. Balaam hit her again forcing her on to the path. Encountering the Angel of the Lord a third time, the donkey fell down under Balaam. Balaam's anger exploded. He hit her again with his staff.

The Lord then enabled the donkey to speak and she turned unto Balaam and said,

"What have I done unto you, that you have hit me these three times?"

Balaam answered, "You have mocked me. If I had a sword, I would kill you right now."

The donkey replied, "Am I not your donkey, upon which you have ridden ever since I was yours up to this day? Did I ever do you wrong?"

Balaam answered, "No."

At this point, The Angel of the Lord interrupts the conversation. He inquires of Balaam on behalf of the donkey. "Why have you hit your donkey three times? I was in the way to stop you from this madness (of pronouncing a curse). Your actions are perverse. The donkey saw me, and she turned away from me three times. Unless she had turned from me, you would have died. Surely, you would have died, but I would have saved her life."

The donkey saw the angel; Balaam did not. (Often times, our pets perceive things we cannot see). The donkey had sense enough to turn away. Balaam was greedy and pursued the matter, cruelly hitting her three times.

God gave the donkey the ability to talk, and explain her actions. The Angel of the Lord defended the donkey. The angel counted the donkey's life worth saving while Balaam deserved to die. God defends animals. Abuse is not his nature.

God counts animal life precious. Ezra 1:6 states: "all the people that gathered about strengthened their hands with vessels of silver, with gold, goods, BEASTS, and precious things." Animals are precious and are included with gold, silver, goods, and precious things.

Proverbs 12:10 states: "A righteous man regards the life of his beast, but the tender mercies of the wicked are cruel". Wicked Balaam thought his actions merciful; they were cruel and thoughtless. God hates cruelty and never condones it.

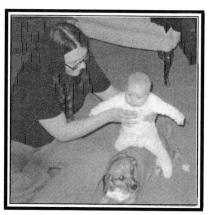

I'm giving baby Renee' her first official ride on Cookie.

God's Provision For Animals
(Psalm 104)

He provides food, shelter, and places of refuge. While riding a four wheel All Terrain vehicle through the fields in back of our farm, Tom came upon a den of foxes. Four babies were safely nestled under a mound of soil surrounded by brush. Mama Fox took advantage of God's provision to keep her family safe and sound.

In the summer I see deer prints around puddles of water. I don't have the responsibility to feed and care for them. They are fed, watered and nurtured by God. He is the one who sends rain and the springs of water into the valleys, which run among the hills to give drink to every beast of the field. The wild animal's thirst is quenched through God's provision.

The fowl of the air are provided with branches, foliage and trees. He causes grass to grow for the cattle to eat and the same grass for birds to make their nests. Tall Fir trees are provided for the stork, blue herons and others to build their nest. High hills are a refuge for wild animals and the rocks hide numerous animal life. Oceans, seas, rivers, and lakes are for the sea creatures to play in. Who would go to all this trouble for creatures of little or no importance?

Night was designed for the animals. At night animals of the forest creep about and seek their prey, they look to God for their food. When the sun goes up, man goes to work and the forest creatures go to bed. Zoos, in order to observe the habits of nocturnal animals, use infrared lights to trick the animals into action. Some are as cute as can be, while others are fierce looking. This time schedule keeps us from bumping into one another—a time for everyone and every creature to work, play and sleep. Psalm 104:20

Winter's belly gets a nice rubdown from me. This was taken on our Michigan farm.

GOD'S VIEW OF ANIMAL CARE

How does God view the life of animals? What about their needs? What are his plans for our pets and animals? He gives us many tips, suggestions, and detailed instructions about the care, safety and intended use of animals.

The following is a list of those detailed instructions, suggestions and tips. In general, our pets and animals care is put into our hands.

Exodus 21:33 says, if a man digs a pit he should cover it, so that an ox or donkey won't fall in.

Exodus 23:4 admonishes people that, if they see their enemies' ox or donkey going astray, they should bring them back to the owner.

Deuteronomy 22:4 says, If we see anyone's beast of burden fallen under the weight of that burden, we ought to help and not turn away.

When plowing, animals must be yoked equally. Don't put an oxen with a donkey. (This clearly puts unnecessary stress on both animals) Deuteronomy 22:10

The plan that man should work six days and rest on the seventh is not for man alone. Deuteronomy 5:14 states, this is so our oxen, donkeys, and cattle may rest as well!

Isaiah 1:3 states, animals have a sense of knowing their master as well as their home.

Exodus 23:11 teaches man to let his field rest after six years of planting on it. The grain left in the field is for the poor, and what they leave is for the beasts of the field to eat.

The life of our pets is precious. Leviticus 24:18 reads, if someone kills one of our animals they are to replace it with like kind.

We may dedicate our animals unto the Lord, if we wish, and they become holy unto Him. Holy is a step above precious. Leviticus 27:28

In Numbers 20:8 when Moses led the children of Israel through the wilderness, God commanded water to be brought forth for the people, <u>as well as for the animals, to drink.</u>

Proverbs 27:23 explains, that God expects us to be diligent in knowing the state of our flocks and looking well to our herds. He wants us to take good care of the animals we have under our dominion. Nothing is worse than a pet owner who lets his animals run wild through the neighborhood expecting others to feed, water and care for them.

Renee' holds her cat Dusty as she climbs the bales of hay in our big 100 year old barn. Dusty came with the farm. Renee' found her in the barn a few days after we moved in. Dusty delivered a litter of kittens on Renee's seventh birthday.

TEN QUESTIONS

God informs Job to learn from the beasts of the field, the fowl of the air, and the fishes of the sea because, they shall declare unto him that they know their lives are from the hand of the Lord. Apparently, our pets have something to say to us. Job 12:7-10.

God asks Job ten questions in regard to the provision and care of animals. God is trying to make a point that people care for their pets, herds, or other animals, but God cares for them all. Put our self in Job's sandals for a moment and try to answer the questions.

1. *Did you give the beautiful feathers unto the peacock or wings that flap proudly to the ostrich?*

2. *Does the eagle mount up at your word to make her nest on high?*

3. *Do you know when the wild goats of the rock will bear young?*

4. *Can you mark when the hinds do calve?*

5. *Who provides for the raven his food?*

6. *Do the lions depend on you to hunt their prey for them?*

7. *Can you fill the appetite of the young lions?*

8.   Were you the one who gave the horse strength, or clothe his neck with thunder?

9.   Can you catch a leviathan with a fishhook or a lasso? (This was a lizard-like creature resembling an enormous crocodile or possibly a dinosaur.)

10.   Look at the behemoth (elephant or hippopotamus), see how he eats grass, his muscles are strong as stones, his bones like bars of iron, he drinks up a river and is in no hurry, who made him Job?

The above conversation shows us that God is watching over and caring for animals. Job 38:41; Job 39: 1, 13, 19, 27-29; Job 40:15-23; Job 41:1

WHO PROVIDES FEED, WATER AND HOUSING?

Job 40:20 states, God made the mountains where all the beasts of the field play. The animals have been given a place to play. Not only do animals work for us but they can play (make merry, rejoice, sport, and laugh) and enjoy life with us.

God preserves man and beast. Their lives are precious to Him. Every thing they need for housing, food, and water has been provided. Psalm 8:7-9.

Psalm 50:11 declares, "I know all the fowl of the mountains and the wild beasts of the field—they are mine!"

Man is still learning about animals but God (intricately) knows them all.

All the animals are supplied with daily food. Psalm 147:9 states, He gives food to the beast and to the young raven that cry.

Luke 12:24: Consider the ravens: they neither sow nor reap; neither do they have storehouses or barns, yet they are fed.

Matthew 10:29: Are not two sparrows sold for a farthing (1 penny)? And one of them shall not fall to on the ground without your Father (God's knowledge). NOT ONE OF THESE are forgotten before God! Our pets that have died are not forgotten before God either. He knows all about them.

Isaiah 43:20: The beast of the field, the dragon and owl will honor him, because he gives them water in the wilderness.

God provides places for animals to bring forth their young. Ezekiel 31:6: ALL the fowl of Heaven build their nests in His boughs. Under His branches ALL the beasts of the field bring forth their young.

An Animal's Heart

Daniel 4:16 presents an interesting account of the madness of Nebuchadnezzar, King of Babylon. His heart changed to the heart of an animal. Heart means inner most understanding and thinking. He was driven from the presence of men, ate grass as ox, his body was wet with the dew, and his body hair grew so that it covered him like feathers on an eagle. His nails grew like birds' claws. Nebuchadnezzar's heart had been changed, and he took on the attributes and understanding of an animal.

People are different from animals, in that animals have a limited capacity for innermost thinking and understanding. Regardless of this difference I find myself talking to my pets all the time. Many times I am sure they understand me even though intellectually I know they do not fully comprehend all I say. Whether I'm happy or sad, I still find release in talking to my pets. God gave them heart to know their response is special.

Not only did God make the animal's heart, but also He put different coverings on different sorts of creatures. Birds have feathers, fish have scales, and our dogs, cats and beasts of the field have fur.

THINGS ANIMALS KNOW

There has been deposited into the heart of animals a knowing of their appointed time (mating season). This is why my family ended up with dozens of kittens and puppies. Jessie would run off in her appointed time, but this was no accidental wandering. She knew her season, and so does your pet. God placed this instinct into their heart.

Some animals know when to go home. After raising chicks in my bathroom for 12 weeks they were put out in the hen house. The first evening I went out to lock them in the hen house. They had me chasing them across the yard. The second night I was delayed in going out to pen them up. It was dusk when I went out and to my surprise they were already in their house asleep on their nests. They came home on their own! This occurrence may be elementary to many, but to a Chicago girl, farm life was like a foreign language. God had put in their heart when to come home, I was not expected to chase them home.

Some of the other animals mentioned in the Bible who come home on their own are the turtle, the crane, and the swallow.

SUBURBS, NOT A NEW IDEA

People, in the last fourty-five years, have moved from cities to the suburbs. This trend toward the promise of a happier and better way of living caught on across the nation. When I was in high school even my family moved from Chicago to the quiet suburbs.

I had just assumed the suburbs were for people until I found verses in Numbers 35:3 and Joshua 21:2 that long ago suburbs had an entirely different purpose. The cities were for people to dwell in, while the suburbs were for their cattle, their goods, and for all their beasts. The suburbs' sole purpose was to house livestock and all other animals. God had a plan for the animals, a home away from the hustle and bustle of the city.

Winter takes a needed siesta on a warm sunny afternoon... Work on the farm is hard!

ANIMALS AT WORK

The history of the Pony Express is taught in junior high school. Today, there is Federal Express, Overnight Express, and so on. Sometimes, we think they were the first to think of this, but not so. There was express mail delivery thousands of years ago. Generally, letters were carried by "speedy footmen" called posts.

In Esther 8:10, there was an urgent need to get letters out across the kingdom. The lives of thousands of people depended upon receiving those letters in time to warn the unsuspecting people their lives were in mortal danger. It was urgent these letters be sent out in time for the people to prepare to defend their lives. These letters weren't carried by foot, but by posts on horseback, mules, camels, and young brood mares called dromedaries.

Animals have been serving humanity for generations. At a time closer to our generation, animals provided other services. Horses pulled milk wagons, ice wagons, fire engines and plows. They delivered things like timber, food, mail, and all sorts of supplies. Animals transported people and their families across prairies and carried men through wars. Other animals, like pigeons, have delivered messages while dolphins and porpoises have chased sharks away from people in the sea.

Dogs are used to lead the blind and listen for the deaf. They sniff out illegal drugs and people who are trapped in buildings or caves. Many dogs such as the St. Bernard have come to the rescue of many an injured or missing skier with the proverbial cask of brandy. Bats gave man the idea for sonar and the birds the idea of flight. We have many things to thank the animals for; we couldn't have accomplished so much without them.

Winter's litter of 5 puppies satisfying their appetites. This looks like an ariel view of cows feeding.

God's Concern Over Lost Pets

Our pets are precious, and when they get lost, our top priority is to find them. Notices get put on telephone poles, and descriptions are placed in the Lost Pet column of local papers. It is not unheard of to leave the family at home by the phone while other members go out to find a lost pet. When we find our pet, we feel like throwing a party. It's wonderful!

The desire to find a lost pet and the anxiety it brings until found reveals the heart of its owner. Likewise, this reveals the heart of the Good Shepherd. Luke 15:4-6 states: "when a shepherd has a flock, and one of the flock gets lost, he will leave the 99 and go into the wilderness to find the lost sheep. When he returns with the sheep, he calls his friends and neighbors to rejoice with him. He found the lost sheep and it's time to celebrate."

There were many sheep in the fold, yet God's concern was for the lost one. We may own several pets yet a lot of concern is exerted to find one that has gotten lost. No effort is too hard or expense too great to bring that lost pet home. The same thought and effort is expressed by the Good Shepherd to bring his lost sheep home. The Good Shepherd is the perfect example of God's concern over the lost.

When our pets get lost we are concerned. God is even more concerned when people are lost in grief, sorrow, pain and despair. He is ever searching to help people just as we search to help our pets. When our pets see us after they have been lost, their tails just about fall off from wagging! They are so happy. What relief. When we encounter the Good Shepherd after floundering in a sea of anger, frustration, fear, or despair, it is a relief to be safe again. It is a picture of how the Good Shepherd cares for us as we care for our pets. God cares about people as well as for animals.

Renee' holds one of Winter's puppies.... But mom I want to keep all of them!

GOD LOVES VARIETY

We are all so different from one another. Animals are too. I've uncovered many varieties mentioned in the Bible. This is only a partial list of actual names I have found:

Hart	Roebuck	Fallow Deer
Wild Goat	Pygarg	Chamois
Wild Ox	Mole	Ferret
Chameleon	Lizard	Snail
Chickens	Coney	Little Owl
Great Owl	Cormorant	Pelican
Gier	Eagle	Hawk
Night Hawk	Cuckoo	Dog
Leopard	Lion	Oxen
Horse	Mule	Donkey
Sheep	Rams	Bruit
Leviathan	Behemoth	Swan
Pelican	Glede	Kite
Vulture	Greyhound	Hare
Raven	Stork	Swine
Heron	Lapwing	Bat
Whales	Fish	Turtledove

Weasel   **Tortoise**   **Mouse**

Wolf   **Boar**   **Quail**

Badger   **Ossifrage**   **Speckled Bird**

Tommy, Renee' and me sitting with Jessie on the farm.

SUMMARY

All the pervious information about animals was found in the Bible. I have not found any other source that builds a more secure foundation regarding animals. When God's previous actions toward animals are revealed we can know his future actions will be the same. God never changes. Hebrews 13:8 states: "He is the same yesterday, today, and tomorrow." With this truth we obtain a firm foundation to build an ark of security and peace about our pets. What God thinks and feels about animals will never change.

The following is a summary of building blocks to understand God's actions and thoughts:

1.   The creation is GOOD

2.   People are given dominion over animals for their own protection and well being

3.   People are given dominion for animal's well being

4.   Animals are worthy of names

5.   Animals are part of God's riches

6.   The promises made to animals by God are kept

7.   Animal abuse is an abomination

8.   All of animal's needs are provided for

9.   Animals are of value

10. Animals have a heart, they experience sadness, pain, loneliness
11. Animals have an innate knowing
12. Cities are for people, suburbs for animals
13. Animals provide service and labor for people
14. Lost pets concern God too
15. God likes variety!

As we step beyond daily life with our pets there is the need for peace after our pets die. The answers we are looking for are just ahead.

Tommy plays in the sand pile while Jessie patrols the grounds on the farm.

One of the 3 litters of puppies from Jessie. Renee' Tommy and me on the farm.

SECTION THREE

ANIMALS IN HEAVEN?

ANIMALS ARE IN HEAVEN

Is it really possible that there are animals in Heaven? In my search for truth I found three examples that set precedence; if God welcomes animals now he will welcome animals later.

First, the book of Revelation 19:14 states, "The armies in Heaven follow Him upon white horses". How many white horses? Jude reveals ten thousands. A vast number of horses now reside in Heaven. A minimum of ten thousands all waiting for a rider!

Second, the prophet Elisha sees horses and chariots of fire in 2 Kings 6:17. Elisha and his servant awake early one morning to find they were surrounded by thousands of the Syrian army who sought their life. The servant was terrified so Elisha asks God to show his servant what else is there.

Suddenly, the young man sees the mountains FULL of horses and chariots of fire now surrounding the Syrian army that was surrounding Elisha. Where did these horses and chariots come from? Heaven.

Third, the prophet Elijah was escorted to Heaven in a chariot drawn by horses of fire. He was standing with Elisha when a whirlwind came down, and the chariot of fire drawn by horses of fire swooped between them, picked up Elijah and vanished. 2 Kings 2:11

What are horses of fire? Horses covered with the glory of God to accomplish a most unique task.

HEAVEN VISITED - ANIMALS SEEN

There are three types of people who have experienced Heaven.

1. Those who have died and returned

2. Those who have died and not returned

3. Those who just visited but not due to death

The apostle Paul wrote in a letter (2 Corinthians 12:2) about entering Heaven but was not sure if he went with his physical body or just left his body for a while and then returned. He saw and talked with Jesus and was sent back to earth to finish the missionary work he was called to do. He did not remain there, it was only a visit. Paul was later martyred at about the age of eighty.

John, one of the twelve disciples, was in prayer on the Lord's day. Suddenly, as he turned around, he realized he was in Heaven. John wrote about what he saw and heard for the future of the world in the book of Revelation. One of the things he saw there was the ten thousands of horses.

John also was not dead but only visiting. John died some time later. He outlived all the other twelve disciples, being the only living disciple left that had experienced first hand the ministry of Jesus.

Paul and John are witnesses that a person doesn't have to die first to go to Heaven. We are offered their testimony the way that a jury hears one's testimony in court today. Witnesses are a valuable commodity. They testify to what they have seen. On the evidence of two or three witnesses a fact is established. If a person has two or three witnesses, he has a very strong case. The Bible states that in the mouth of two or three witnesses every word is established as fact. Presently, there are at least three witnesses alive on the earth today who have gone to Heaven and come back. A fourth witness went to Heaven, came back, wrote a book, and passed away later on. The following is a retelling of their Heavenly encounters.

Jessie with her look of "Won't you please pet me now?" Jessie is in Heaven right now where she is getting all the petting she wants.

WITNESS ONE - MRS. SPRINGER*

Mrs. Springer was traveling abroad, away from friends and family when she became ill. Her physical health deteriorated to the point in which she straddled between earth and Heaven. One morning, while looking out the window she saw her late brother-in-law who had previously died, standing there. He escorted her to Heaven. She was told that when she was stronger she could come back.

Soon upon her arrival in Heaven, she came upon her family's collie dog, Sport. He was tumbling and rolling in the grass with some children. When the dog saw her, he bounded over and fawned at her feet. She threw her arms around him. His coat was silkier than silk. Her brother-in-law commented that Sport seemed to understand every word she said.

Mrs. Springer recalled to him why Sport deserved to be there. His master, a young child, was crossing the rail road tracks when a train was heard approaching. Sport heard the train too and thought the child was in danger. Not knowing any better, and with the safety of the boy on his mind, the dog ran after him. The boy lived, but the train hit Sport.

Mrs. Springer's pleasure was obvious when seeing Sport again. She thought it right, a pet so faithful, should be in Heaven waiting his master's arrival. This is just one of many of the sweet proofs she found of the Father's care; the things that give people enjoyment on earth are found in Heaven.

Mrs. Springer also recalled seeing a little girl she recognized that had died and gone to Heaven. The grief-stricken family had worried that their child lacked family members in Heaven to meet or greet her upon arrival. They had no idea that Jesus himself had taken personal care of her. While the shy little girl sat on Jesus' lap, a white Angora kitten, which belonged to the youngster on earth, bounded in, jumped in her lap and fell asleep. Back on earth this kitten had turned up missing, the family never knowing what happened to it. This little girl hugged and kissed her kitten with great joy.

This act of Heavenly love helped her adjust to the new surroundings of Heaven. The confidence she felt upon the arrival of her kitten gave her what she needed to begin playing with the other children.

When Mrs. Springer returned to earth she visited with the parents of that little girl. She told them their little daughter was doing beautifully, and that she had her white angora kitten there with her. They need not grieve nor worry any longer. The Lord was taking well care of their child.

From MY DREAM OF HEAVEN by Rebecca Springer

WITNESS TWO - BETTY MALZ*

Betty died from a burst appendix. The gangrene spread throughout her body. All her organs shut down one after the other until she died. Not long after death, her father had come to the hospital to visit her unaware she had died. He began to speak to her in the name of Jesus when suddenly; she sat up, alive and totally recovered. When she was in Heaven she was so comfortable in the presence of God's home (Heaven) she wrote a book telling about this experience. Although she did not personally see any animals, she was so very aware of joy and happiness there that she was sure if we needed or wanted our pets, they would be there.

She relates that she heard from one person who died and was in Heaven, that there were little children laughing, running about, catching tiny birds in their hands, singing and playing with ANIMALS. There was plenty of countryside for animals to dwell in. This person felt sure that the animals were not in the city section of the capital but in the countryside.

*From HEAVEN A BRIGHT AND GLORIOUS PLACE by Betty Malz

WITNESS THREE - ROBERTS LAIRDON*

Roberts Lairdon went for a visit to Heaven when he was eight years old. He was raised in a family where prayer and reading the Bible were strongly impressed upon him. One summer afternoon he went into his bedroom to read his Bible. There, his spirit left his body and went to Heaven. Roberts saw many new things there such as, streets paved with transparent gold, and gates made of one pearl. He also saw things very similar to that of earth, such as people, buildings, natural wonders, and ANIMALS.

All types of animals, from 'a to z'. He saw a dog, a goat, birds, and a lion. There were other forms of animal life there also, but he was unable to identify them as he saw them from a distance. He did notice, however, that the animals did not run from people, nor did they attack them. The animals were calm and peaceful.

From I SAW HEAVEN by Roberts Lairdon

WITNESS FOUR – JESSE DUPLANTIS*

Rev. Duplantis is a world renowned Evangelist who was visiting a church in Magnolia, Arkansas in August 1988. As he was sitting in a restaurant with the pastor of the church that he was visiting, he felt compelled to go back to his hotel room. When he got back to his room he placed a "Do Not Disturb" sign on the door, took off his coat and then knelt down beside the bed to pray. All of a sudden he felt himself being pulled up out of the room. When he looked up he noticed that he was sitting in something resembling a chariot. After what seemed to him to be only a short time the door opened and then he realized that he was in Heaven. When he stepped out and began to look around he had this to say:

"It was a beautiful land. Trees were lined up alongside the River of Life as it flowed throughout Paradise. Thousands of people were standing around under the trees. They all and been brought there in those chariot-like vehicles, the same as I was.

I had always thought that everybody who went to Heaven was grown up. But I saw children too. I also noticed horses, dogs and large cats like lions."

Rev. Duplantis then went on to see other wonderful works that God has prepared for those who believe. In a discussion with one of the patriarchs of the Old Testament Mr. Duplantis was told:

> *"Jesse, the earth is God's creation. His taste there (Earth) is His taste here (Heaven). Every desire you could possibly think of has been met to your specifications for your home, plus God put a few of His own."*

Think about that statement for a minute. If pets and animals are on earth and earth is just a taste of Heaven then it would be only reasonable to **EXPECT YOUR PETS AND OTHER ANIMALS** to be in Heaven too!

*From HEAVEN: CLOSE ENCOUNTERS OF THE GOD KIND by Jesse Duplantis

How Animals Get From Earth To Heaven

When we talk breath is released. Sometimes this is evident when someone who is intent on talking takes a deep breath before continuing on. When God speaks breath comes out of his mouth only his breath has the power to bring life into existence. Humans can resuscitate another to life but cannot create life with our breath. It is with the breath of life that God created everything including the animals. When pets or other animals die that "breath of life" returns to God. Psalm 104:29, 30 state: God receives their breath and they die and God sends forth his Spirit (breath) and they are created. Their bodies die, but their uniqueness, personality, vivaciousness and vitality return to Him.

When our pets die we experience feelings of loss and grief. Even when I see wild animals that have been hit by vehicles lying by the side of the road I feel pain and sorrow in my heart. How much more grief and loss is felt when our pets die. A valuable part of our life is missing. The companionship, friendship and comfort found with our pet is no longer there. There is comfort though, because as sensitive as we are to the loss there is another even more sensitive. God.

Matthew 10:29 states: not even one sparrow falls to the ground without God's knowledge. This verse tells me God is very sensitive. His awareness of all life is extremely heightened. How can God know when even a sparrow falls to the ground? The breath of that bird returns to him in the same way as the breath of our pets and other animals.

God understands the feelings of loss and loneliness we have. We do not suffer alone. He also knows the difference between the wild animal and our precious pets that are of great value to us. Because he knows the difference, he is able to keep our pets for us in Heaven. The pets we love and enjoy here will be there, kept for us because God cares about you and me and our pets.

Rocky, Tommy's pet rat. This is the one I gave C.P.R. to. Boy oh boy -- a mom's job is never too small.

COME, LET US REASON TOGETHER

Some people think reason and the Bible do not mix. God calls people to come and reason with him in Isaiah 1:18. God does remind us his reasoning is higher than ours but, he is still open to reason with us and bring us new ideas and a higher way of thinking and living. Why is God so interested in what people think as well as their needs and desires? Why are we interested in our children's thoughts, needs and desires? Love.

Reason: When my daughter Renee' was nine she received a doll house kit from grandma. The picture on the box showed a lovely doll house, only someone had to put it together. That someone turned out to be dad. Every night he drove an hour to get home from work. He ate dinner and sat down to piece together the doll house. Hours, days, weeks went by. At last, the doll house was finally finished. Tom had no interest in doll houses. He had no desire to use his free time to build one. The doll house was for Renee' and the driving force was love. It was important to Renee'; therefore, important to her dad.

Eventually Renee's interests changed. The doll house was replaced with drums and boys. In fact, several years later, Renee's brother, Tommy "blew up" the doll house with fireworks one Forth of July.

If Tom went to all that trouble to build a doll house only to have it blown up later, wouldn't God, whose love for us is so much greater than our love for our children, allow our pets in Heaven?

Just like Tom supplied Renee's desire, God wants to supply ours. Pets in our lives are not paramount to survival on earth. It is not crucial to have a pet to just exist. Pets were created to take us beyond just mere existence to wonderfully supply a need for people to express and receive love without rejection.

Reason: Moms and dads bring home pets for their children. Why? We like to see our children happy. It pleases parents when their children take pleasure in their pets. God is a father. He loves to see his children enjoy things, also. The pleasure he receives from our enjoyment is like the pleasure we received when Tom finished the doll house or when we brought home a cat or dog for the kids.

Renee' was in second grade when she went out to catch the bus for school. Suddenly, I heard her screaming "Love is dead!" "Love is dead!" I thought, "love's not dead, what a strange thing to say". I ran outside and down the driveway. There was Love, her cat, lying by the side of the road. I sent her on to school, but a plan formed in my mind that I was determined to carry out.

I went to the local pound and bought another cat. An orange tomcat we named Glory. I drove directly to the school. I stopped briefly at the office and went to Renee's classroom. Renee' was very surprised to see me standing in her classroom holding a big orange cat. She jumped up from her seat, took the cat in her arms and cuddled him close. She was so happy. The pleasure on her face did so much for me. To see her happy again was paramount in my mind and brought me such pleasure.

It pleased this parent to see her daughter happy! This type of concern and love is in God. His love for us doesn't fade away; it is infinite and goes beyond pets dying, our dying and on into eternity where he has reserved a place for our pets and us.

Reason: If you, like I, need the company, joy and happiness our pets bring to be satisfied in Heaven then God will extend the time and effort to see that your pet is there. That's how important your happiness and pleasures are to him.

Reason: I like the answer Billy Graham's wife gave him about Heaven. Billy Graham, as you probably know is our generation's most accepted and well-known Evangelist. His schedule is one that would wear out a twenty five-year-old man in a month or two not to mention a man in his mid eighties.

Billy came home after a long series of preaching crusades around the world. Upon arrival in the States, he was called on to fulfill duties waiting for him. He was tired and needed a well-deserved rest. There just wasn't time to take that rest.

One of the ways he liked to relax was to play golf. The problem was, there was seldom time to play. In fact, it was so seldom he couldn't even justify owning a set of clubs. One day as he was preparing to leave for an appointment he asked his wife if she thought God would have golf courses in Heaven.

Taking a moment to think, her response was something like, "Billy, when we get to Heaven and you need to play golf to be fully satisfied and happy, then God will surely have a golf course waiting for you."

Even if he was the only one to ever use it, God would have it for him just to see him happy and fulfilled. That answer describes God and his love for us to a TEE. She couldn't have answered him better or more accurately than she did.

We can definitely know that our pets and other animals will be in Heaven if for no other reason than this one. You are no less important to God than Billy Graham is.

Jessie poses with Tommy, cousin Margo and Renee'.

HEAVEN THE ORIGINAL
EARTH THE PATTERN

Heaven is the original, and Earth is the pattern of it. Heaven operates above the speed of light while everything on earth operates at or below the speed of light. This is why we cannot see Heaven unless God should open the eyes of our understanding. Earth operates at and below the speed of light.

Hebrews 9:23, states "the patterns of things in the Heavens" needed to be purified. These patterns are the original; earth holds the duplicates. When I sew, I use patterns from Vogue, Simplicity, or McCall's. The store does not sell me the original pattern, but a copy. The pattern makers keep the original in a safe place.

On several occasions I have sat with Tommy and helped him put together model airplanes and ships. These models are built to scale and will not be the size of the original. If there is a lifeboat placed on the bow of the model then that's where it is on the original. The decals are placed on the model exactly where they are placed on the prototype. Earth is like that model plane or boat with Heaven being the original.

Heaven is the original pattern for the things on earth. Either through travel or books about the world it is apparent there are many different people, wondrous sights, and unusual animals. Those things we see here are the pattern of what is already waiting for us in Heaven. God is not a respecter of persons, places or animals. He is interested in all people and all animals. The difference being, people have a choice of whether or not to come to him. With this choice hanging in the balance, God will accept all who come to him (see section 5 Getting to Heaven). Animals however, are not required to make a choice and are always received by him. I believe we will be surprised at the number of animals in Heaven, some we have seen before and can identify, and others we have never known. With earth being the pattern we can determine there is no boredom in the realm of Heaven simply by looking at the variety of animals on earth.

Many things we have here can also be found in Heaven, such things as doors, gates, walls, houses, mansions, water, lakes, rivers, streets, trees, grass, flowers, mountains, and forests. A good question to ask ourselves is "Why would God put in Heaven grass, flowers, bushes and trees, things a lot of people dislike to maintain, and ignore our pets, a very significant part of our lives?"

Doctor Percy Collett, a missionary to the Amazon, visited Heaven for 'five and one half earth days'. He had prayed for several years to see Heaven. That request was answered. When he came back, he recorded the experience on a series of tapes.

He reported Heaven, to be similar to planet Earth but at least 80 times larger than Earth. He saw the city that God is preparing in Heaven, 1,200 miles wide, 1,200 miles long and 1,200 miles high. A city that large would take up most of the United States—just a city!

God patterned earth after his dwelling place and has included our beloved pets. He made earth to house his creation and Heaven to hold them until we arrive.

It should also be noted that Dr. Collett witnessed animals too. He saw thousands and thousands of turtledoves, some of which, the children played with.

Jessie gives her favorite cat, Praise, her morning bath.

Barney is on the job monitoring the front lawn.

Barney is doing her daily sit-ups to stay in shape.

SECTION FOUR

HOW TO RECOVER FROM A PET'S DEATH

COMFORT THROUGH VISION

Visual aid is an important key to comfort. We are going to use what our 'witnesses' saw in Heaven and what the Bible says is there to build a vision. With Earth being a replica of Heaven it is easier to understand what is there for us. Picture in your mind a dozen or more trees laden with delicious fruit growing next to the crystal clear water flowing peacefully past your mansion. See your beloved pet or animal friend sitting on the polished marble stairs at the entrance to your mansion. They are waiting for you.

You are walking up the pearly sidewalk laid between lush foliage and perfect trees. Every leaf and blade of grass is delicately formed in place and greener than green. Delicate flowers, brilliant with hues of color are splashed throughout the grass. These flowers gently spill delicate fragrances superior to those on earth. There is no evidence anywhere of spoilage. Everything you see and everywhere you look is the beauty of perfection.

Your pet has seen you approaching! It is standing up, ears perked, tail wagging or is purring and making meowing twittering sounds. You kneel down. The cat stretches before bounding into your arms while the dog barks and runs and licks your hands and face then runs in circles with joy. It's your pet or other animal friend, but there is no trace of any illness, infirmity, or old age, only perfection.

It is wonderful how the two of you seem to communicate like never before. Your pet seems to let you know how happy it is to see you again. You hold that beloved pet closely and run your hands over the exquisitely soft fur. Your pet nuzzles your face and licks your nose. You burst with laughter, and set your pet back down on the pearly walk. It's true! What seemed to have been lost has been kept exclusively for you. You're together again! You and your pet walk into your mansion where all of you will live together forever.

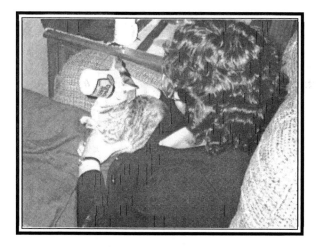

Help!! I've fallen in this cup and I can't get out. I discovered this day that Praise likes cheese -- very, very much.

How To Use Your Vision

When sorrow or grief want to swallow you up, replace those thoughts with the above vision of Heaven. Imagine you feel the smooth, cool, pearly sidewalk under your feet. Now you are stepping onto the velvety, soft grass. Imagine the soft grass between your toes and under your bare feet. Pick a delicate, fragrant flower; let the smooth petals touch your cheek. See your pet in your arms, well and happy. Your pet wants to smell the flower and you let it. The two of you are doing things together again. **No longer think of your animal friend as just being in your past, but think of them now being in your future.**

Imagine your pet dancing happily about your feet or rubbing against your ankles with greetings of love. Remember the feel of the soft fur against your ankles and between your fingers, the soft tongue on your face, or the sandpaper tongue on your cheek. You are together again and no one or no thing can change that. Think the vision until you are peaceful again. Do this as often as you like. No one has to know what you're thinking about if you don't want to tell anyone.

You can also support another who is grieving with this same method. Help them along in the visualization giving them the picture you have in your heart. Let them know how wonderful it will be to have their pet back in their arms again. Talk it over with them as often as they need to hear it. Think about how you would have felt if someone had talked to you with a vision of Heaven. Comfort and hope will well up inside them. They will be on the road to recovery and you will have been an immense help.

If you are having trouble imagining things in Heaven, refer to Section Three, Heaven the original, Earth the pattern. The truth is, what we find here is in Heaven, with the exception that there is NO deterioration, NO decay, and NO death. There is NO sorrow or tears, only joy, peace, fulfillment and contentment.

Praise peers out from her favorite Lay-Z-Boy chair to see what is going on.

EXPLAINING THE DEATH
OF A PET TO CHILDREN

The difficulty of explaining death is highly exaggerated. If you are like me and have jumped to this chapter because you need a quick answer, I suggest, after reading this section, you go back and read the rest of the book. Only a good foundation will be able to support the walls of knowledge.

Sit down in a quiet spot with the child and tell them you will explain what happened to their pet. Use the following visual aids to help them understand death. If you have a hand puppet available, put it on your hand. Your hand brings the puppet to life. When your hand moves inside, the puppet appears to take on 'life'. The puppet is animated by the move of your hand. It takes on whatever personality, movement, or character you choose. Show the child how the puppet moves. Its mouth opens and closes; it can tickle the child or pull on the child's shirt. Take your hand out of the puppet. It lies motionless. It has no life in it anymore. It is dead so to speak. The source of its 'life' (your hand) has been removed and it has 'died'. Your pet's source of life was not a hand but a spirit created by God. When that spirit of life departed, it returned to the One who gave it, God.

For the next demonstration you will need a sweater or jacket. Lay the sweater on a chair or sofa. Be sure the child notices that the sweater does not move. It has no 'life' of its own.

Put the garment on now. Illustrate how the sweater has taken on your shape, form, and movement. If you are swinging your arms, the sweater swings too. If you are fat or thin, the sweater looks fat or thin. In fact, the sweater is similar to our skin that takes on the same shape, form, and movement of our body.

Remove the sweater. Have the child notice that the sweater no longer has any movement. The form and shape of your body no longer exist in that sweater. The fibers have relaxed and returned to their original shape. It could be said that the sweater has 'died'. All animals, fish, and birds have a spirit. When that spirit leaves their body it returns to the One who created it. Their body was only the house for their spirit. The animal has left its body and gone to Heaven where God lives.

BriteBooks and I have created a very special children's Coloring /Activity Book to help a child recover from the loss of a pet. It is designed to give the child an opportunity to talk about the pet or animal friend that went to Heaven while coloring and doing the activities. You will find this is a wonderful time to encourage them to share their feelings from grief or sadness and talk about seeing their pet again in Heaven. I believe you will find much value in this very useful and comforting tool. *(Please see the last page of this book for ordering information).*

God Is Love?

It is significant for a child to know that the God of the Bible is not responsible for taking away a loved pet. 1John 4:8 states, "God is Love". When my nine-year-old son's pet lab rat, Rocky, died, I wanted him to know God did not kill it. God is life and there is no death in him. Acts 17:25 states "…seeing he gives to all life, and breath and all things…" He cannot dispense what he does not have, namely death. (Now, you might just be wondering "how is it then there is death"? The answer to that is Romans 6:23.)

It was a quiet Saturday afternoon. Without warning, I was alerted to Tommy's anxious cry that there was a problem. I went up to his room where he showed me Rocky, who was staggering around in her cage. He was afraid for her and it showed.

I picked up the rat and held her in my hands. She seemed to be having a hard time breathing, and she lay so still. I proceeded to give her mouth to mouth resuscitation (parents are known to go 'above and beyond their call of duty' when their children are afraid and crying). I blew into her little mouth and gently pushed on her little chest, again and again. Rocky did not revive but died in my hands. Tommy broke down crying. His heart was hurting and so was mine. We cried together. I've never cried over a rat's death before or since then!

Taking hold of my emotions and gaining some control, I thought, 'if I took desperate measures to revive Rocky, then God, who loved Tommy more than I, would take measures to keep Rocky in Heaven for him.

Psalms 139:17-18 states, "God thinks of us even while we sleep. His thoughts of us are greater than the grains of sand found on earth". I freely admit I didn't think of that lab rat every day and as much as I love my son my thoughts are not always centered on him. But, God's thoughts are. They are centered on you, too.

God's interest in Tommy and Rocky the rat far exceeded mine. I told this to Tommy in a way a nine-year-old could understand. His crying subsided as he listened.

Furthermore, I told him that Rocky was in Heaven with Jesus, the One who made all things for us to enjoy. I went to the bookshelf, took down a picture Bible and showed him drawings of Jesus loving the children with animals all around. A picture is worth a thousand words. He saw that Jesus loved children, and that their hurts are important to him.

He understood that since Jesus loved him, God also cared about his pet. The life, personality, and character of Rocky had come from God and gone back to God. Rocky was with Jesus. When Tommy goes to Heaven, Rocky will be there, waiting for him.

Romans 8:32 states, He that spared not his Son, but delivered him up for us all, how shall he not with him also freely give us all things? Simply speaking, God gave Jesus, His own dear son, for us. So why keep a lab rat from Heaven when she gave so much enjoyment and companionship to Tommy?

It is God's greatest desire that everyone understands and absolutely knows the length, depth, breadth, and height of the love of Jesus Christ. Tommy received comfort knowing Jesus loved him, loved Rocky, and loved me. Yes, Yes... God is Love!

Renee' and Tommy take turns hugging Praise.

Handling The Fear of Death

While working at the local library, a woman came in looking for a book to explain the death of pets to a child. The families' pet pony had died. Her four-year-old son was terrified that mom was next to die! I looked through the card catalogue and went to several shelves looking for a suitable book. As we searched, I told her about this book which I was writing at the time. She left the library empty handed, urging me on with, "Hurry and write your book."

Children, like this woman's four-year-old, are looking for some answers. They hurt as much as adults and want to be comforted. There are steps we can take to alleviate the dread and fear of death in children. Like a surgeon, we can immediately and skillfully remove that fear and dread.

Giving a hug to the child is a good place to start. Loving, physical contact fosters a feeling of understanding and security. The hurting child knows that you love them when they're hugged. This demonstration of love depicts God's nature.

If the child is able to do any counting ask them to count to eighty. If they can only count to ten, help them to fill in the rest. It is a clear picture of how far away eighty is from your age. Why do this? God promises long life to people. Psalm 90:10 says, the days of our years are seventy, if we are strong, eighty. Psalm 91:16 promises, if we are not satisfied with life at eighty, we can live even longer. Your child will soon realize you are not going to die too, that you will stay until satisfied. You have God's word on it. John 10:10 states, "I am come that you might have life and that life more abundantly."

For additional reinforcement any picture books of Jesus with children will help. Sit with the child and point out Jesus with the little children on his lap, in his arms, and standing all-round Him. Mention the different children, trees, or birds in the picture. Point out; "See how Jesus loves the children? He loves you too." The picture of love and concern will comfort their heart. When we approach this subject with wisdom and tenderness children tend toward a very positive response.

... And why can't I come in through the window? Praise.

How To Conduct A Funeral For Your Pet

When a pet has been a faithful friend and companion, it is good to give them a proper burial. The formality of this helps us in many ways. There is the release and closure that promotes emotional healing. There is the realization that our pet is not going to be here with us anymore, but has gone to Heaven. On occasion when we happen upon the burial site it seems to trigger the memory of that beloved pet and the bittersweet memories connected with it. Conducting a funeral will bring comfort as we remember former days while understanding our pet is in Heaven.

At the grave site a dedication or few words spoken is recommended. Often times a pet's death is sudden and unexpected and we have not had an opportunity to say any parting words. At the funeral, when we say those parting words the healing from separation begins to bring closure

What my children and I did was write out one or two things we especially remembered with that pet and then read them. Most of the time words flowed out as our emotions were released. I would encourage you to do the same. Cry and release the emotions you are experiencing. Let the pain in your heart come out. If you feel angry that your pet died, then say so. If you are deeply grieved then say so. This is YOUR funeral service, and you can have it any way you want. Your thoughts and feelings are important so don't hold back. There is no wrong thing to say or do. There is no one to condemn your words or actions. Your pet and you had a special relationship, and you have the right to show it. You loved your pet, so don't hesitate to express that love.

I encourage you though, to end your dedication with similar words that Tommy and I said when Rocky died. We went away from the funeral with a definite picture instilled: there is another joyous day coming when we will be with our pets again. Remember, an animal friend that has past away is not lost to us, but they are in our future, waiting for us in Heaven.

This is what we said:

> *"Dear Jesus, We want to thank you for all the enjoyable times Tommy had with Rocky. We know she is in Heaven with you. Thank you for taking care of her until we come to Heaven, too. Rocky was a good pet and we will miss her but, we know she is with you. Amen."*

Tommy never cried again after that day. He has never mentioned her death or how much he missed her. Not because he doesn't remember her, but because he has been healed inside. He is a happy, well-adjusted young man who knows his pet rat is in Heaven. He doesn't have to be sad any more. He has let joy be his strength. You can be joyful too; not because your pet is gone, but because you know where your pet is and that you will be together again. I believe that when you do these simple steps you will experience the same comfort. Knowing what to do in this delicate and sensitive matter brings the peace and comfort we seek.

How many more days until I can open this? Even the pets get Christmas gifts in our family. Barney.

When A Pet Is "Put To Sleep"

Having to decide the fate of a beloved pet is a traumatic act. So many uneasy thoughts, guilt, remorse, dread, fear, heartache, loneliness, just to name a few, run through the mind. How can we deal with these very real feelings and thoughts?

A veterinarian can only give us options. We must make the final decision. Seeing our pet suffering, whether from an accident, old age, or illness is difficult to bear. Letting them die with dignity is even harder. Maybe they will recover. Maybe they will get worse. Take the time to get more than one opinion from reputable veterinarians. Weigh the facts like a balance. When one side tips greater than the other does you have a pretty good idea of what to decide.

By this time I sincerely hope you are well convinced that animals and other pets go to Heaven. As hard as your decision must be, there is comfort knowing you will see your pet again. This is not your final good bye. The sting of death has been vanquished.

I remember when my friend Dorothy called me about her dog Tinkerbell. She was not sure if she could 'put her to sleep'. Tinkerbell was very old, and difficult to manage and care for. She didn't want to be a "bad" person and wanted to do the right thing. We discussed many of the things written in this book.

That was many years ago. I remember telling her about writing this book and her encouraging words to me. She expressed how much the advice and comfort she received gave her the courage to make the right decision. She couldn't have done it if she hadn't known Tinkerbell was in Heaven and in her future.

Two naps for the price of one. Barney takes a nap on Renee'.

JESSIE GOES TO HEAVEN

Now it was my turn to take my own advice and practice what I "preached".

It was the beginning of fall when I stubbornly acknowledged Jessie had some very real medical problems. Her failing eyesight coupled with deafness considerably hindered our relationship with her. After discussing with Tom about putting her down I was put in the position as the one who should take her. No one else had the fortitude (as it was put) to "drive her to her death". The night before she was scheduled for "departure" I tenderly talked with her while brushing her to look pretty for Heaven. That was when I closely observed how bony thin she had become in the past couple of weeks. She gave off a very unpleasant odor, which I suspected was from cancer.

The morning had come and I braced myself for the unpleasant task ahead. I fastened her collar, which she seldom wore. It was very big on her. She had lost significant weight, but being a sheltie, it was hard to see with all her fur. I put her in the car. If there had been any way to prolong her life I would have wholeheartedly done it at once. There wasn't.

It was so hard walking her inside knowing what was ahead. Before she was taken, I kissed her and told her good-bye, but not forever. I told her I would see her again. When the doctor came and walked her away I knew I would never forget her expression and demeanor. Utter sadness. She hung her head, walked away dejected and defeated. I felt like a traitor to a wonderful friend. I hated death and what it does to the living. I wanted to run and scoop her up and take her back home. I could not. I loved her so much. Crying, I turned around and left.

I never had the opportunity for a funeral nor for a burial site. I regret that. Of all the pets we had Jessie deserved this the most but got the least. I don't know what was done with her body and I never got her collar back. For quite some time I felt in limbo, but now I am resolved, I will see her in Heaven and she won't be angry with me. When we meet again we will take up our relationship just as if it never had been interrupted. She is in my future.

When I watch old family movies (now on video) and see her young, vital and full of life, and compare it with how weary and sick she was on her last day I know I made the right decision. She is waiting at my mansion's doorstep in wonderful, beautiful Heaven, very alive and kept by God for me.

Chirps the Robin

A few years ago Renee' rescued a baby robin from the middle of a busy road. When we weren't out buying worms at the bait shop we were digging them up at the local park. Chirps needed numerous feedings a day until she was able to fly away on her own. I think Chirps is the only robin with an angel assigned to keep her safe. We look for her every spring.

Renee' hand feeds Chirps one of the hundreds of worms needed to make her grow.

Renee' visits Chirps in our basement where she grew up until she could fly. Renee' is explaining to Chirps how to be a bird.

Renee' takes Chirps outside for a test flight. It was a number of weeks later before she flew away.... We were running out of worms.

SECTION FIVE

How To Live With Your Pet Forever

GETTING TO HEAVEN

Pets and animals go directly to Heaven. It is not required for pets and animals to choose where they want to go when they die. It is different for people. God gives people the freedom to choose where they want to spend eternity. God loves people so much, he won't force any decision upon them. People were made with the capacity to understand Heaven, animals were not.. People are a higher class of species than animals in that they have the ability and power to choose and speak words. Animals were not given this privilege nor were they given the freedom to choose their eternity by words. Our pets go directly to Heaven and God takes the responsibility for having them waiting there for us. The question remains "are our pets waiting for us in vain"?

So, how do people get to Heaven?" Our pets are there, and we want to be with them. We can't fly there. We can't take a rocket ship there. Our pets are there, and we want to be with them. Don't be dismayed. God has a plan all worked out just for you and me. We can follow the plan like an architect follows a blueprint to build a house. If the architect follows the blueprint, there will be a house. If we follow God's blueprint, we'll have Heaven as our home.

To begin, God loves all people. God is not angry with me or you or anyone for that matter. Believe it or not, there is no record in Heaven of anyone's sins, deliberate or accidental. They have all been blotted out. Whew! The sins of the whole world are canceled, and the slate wiped clean. All those things, past, present and future have been forgiven. God is not holding anything against you or me. This puts us on talking terms with God, but what do we say to him?

Where do we begin? Tell God you want to choose Heaven as your eternal destination. The bridge that opens communication between you and God is Jesus Christ who paid for and canceled all our sins, debts and trespasses through his death on the cross. Because of what Jesus did for us we can spend eternity in Heaven. We can't get there by our own efforts, no matter how good and wonderful we are. Which by the way, is good news, because if I couldn't earn Heaven by good works then I can't lose Heaven by bad works. Jesus has taken care of that. Pray the following prayer. God is waiting for us to make a decision. Your pet is waiting for you to make a decision. From the heart pray out loud:

"God in Heaven, thank you for what Jesus did for me. I believe Jesus is your Son and that you have raised him from the dead. I invite Jesus to come into my life and my heart to live forever. Thank you for coming to live in my heart, for making a home for me in Heaven and preparing a place where I can go to be with You and my beloved pets. Amen."

Children often want to invite Jesus into their hearts also. They have so much trust. When Tommy was four years old, I asked him if he would like to invite Jesus into his heart. He did. Your child can pray the simple prayer Tommy prayed.

> *"Jesus, I want you to come and live in my heart. Thank you for coming in. I love You, Amen".*

Why not ask yourself and your child if they would like to invite Jesus into their heart? He stands at the door of every man, woman, boy and girl's heart knocking, waiting for them to open the door to invite Him in. It is the beginning to that abundant life of peace and joy. Children respond so quickly to Jesus' invitation—we have much to learn from them!

God has made it easy for us to get to Heaven. Receive Jesus in our heart. Our words (prayer) lets God know we have chosen His offer of Heaven.

Tell someone about your decision to choose Heaven. Share with them the hope and comfort of God for you and for them. Write me and let me know. I have some special booklets I want to send you free of charge as a gift.

You can contact me by E-mail at: crwebb@britebooks.org or by writing to: BriteBooks Dept. 11, P.O. Box 801, Ortonville, MI 48462-0801

This would be a great time for you to fill out one of the certificates shown on page 104-107.

SECTION SIX

FINAL THOUGHTS

Help For Sick And Injured Pets

I trust you have not skipped your opportunity to go to Heaven. This chapter is just for you who have taken God's offer. One of the benefits (beside Heaven) is, those who are now "in Christ Jesus" are new creatures (on the inside) and Heaven has imparted healing and power from God through us to lay hands on the sick and see them recover. This privilege is not just for sick people but for animals as well.

In July 1988, a horse Jessie had decided to chase kicked her. She ran beside the horse barking. A second later the horse kicked her with the rear hoof. It tore a very large hole in Jessie's side. We spoke the name of Jesus over her while we rushed her to the Vet. While he checked her out, we continued to pray for her total healing. We were certain she would recover. Remarkably, there had not been any broken bones or torn muscles. She just needed stitching up.

When we returned to the Vet the next day, we learned she had needed over forty stitches. She was home for only a couple of days when the skin that was bruised around the stitching began to tear away. Jessie ended up with the skin on the right side having a hole the size of a dinner plate. Considering the size of a sheltie this wound looked formidable. We coupled the practical with the supernatural. We laid our hands on her head and believed for her recovery as well as cleansing the wound daily.

There was no negative talk permitted concerning Jessie. When the kids wanted to cry and bemoan her we hushed them. She was going to recover, period. The veterinarian said the wound wouldn't be closed until January, and about six months after that she might have fur again. We heard him, but we knew Jessie would recover much sooner than that. We had prayed, there was no other alternative.

At Thanksgiving, four months after the accident, her wound was totally closed. Any evidence of an injury was completely covered with fur. Jessie had fully recovered and was back to her happy frisky self.

You can do the same for your pets. They will respond to your prayers. Out pets depend on us for so much. They want to be well and we can do more than be just a spectator of our pet's suffering.

Hey!!! Who let the goats out? This was my first and last experience with goats. Boy are they friendly.

THE FUTURE FOR ANIMALS

God also has a plan for animals. There is an age yet to come in which animals will play a big part. Ten thousands of white horses will carry an army into battle. After this battle there is a millennium (1,000 years) of peace and restoration in the earth. Then God will make a covenant with the beasts of the field, the fowl of Heaven, and the creeping things of the ground. They shall lie down in safety. The bow and sword of war will cease, (Hosea 2:18). The wolf and the lamb shall feed together. The lion shall eat straw like the ox, and dust shall be the serpent's meat. The leopard shall lie down with the kid. The calf shall lie down with the young lion and the stall-fed animals. The cow and the bear shall feed together. Their young ones shall lie down together. None of these animals shall hurt or destroy. (Isaiah 11:6-9)

Another day is coming when people shall come into Zion flowing together to the goodness of the Lord, for wheat, wine, oil, the young of the flock, and for the herd. Their soul shall be watered as a garden, and their soul shall not sorrow any more, at all. God includes ANIMALS in this rejoicing and eternal absence of sorrow (Jeremiah 31:12).

This is the future for animals, what about yours?

Epilogue

Our pets are waiting for us to join them in Heaven. That decision is ours. The good things Heaven has in store for all people can only be totally realized when we arrive there, but one thing is for sure, our pets and other animal friends will be there to welcome us home to live with them forever.

If you have decided to go to Heaven because of this book please write and let me know. If you have been comforted or have questions or additional ideas, please write me. I would love to hear from you. Every attempt will be made to answer your letters and E-mails.

You can contact me by E-mail at: crwebb@britebooks.org or by writing to: BriteBooks Dept. 11, P.O. Box 801, Ortonville, MI 48462-0801

Finally, you can be sure I will be in Heaven. You will know me, I'll be the one with the black Siamese in my arms, and the sheltie lying by my feet.

Reading Suggestions

Angels Watching Over Me, by Betty Malz

My glimpse of Eternity, by Betty Malz

Heaven: Close Encounters of The God Kind, by Jesse Duplantis

Bibliography & Contacts

Lairdon, Roberts. I saw Heaven
Albury Publishing 1995
http://www.robertsliardon.org/

Malz, Betty. Heaven a Bright and Glorious Place.
Old Tappen, New Jersey: Fleming H. Revell
Company, 1989.
http://www.bibleprobe.com/my_glimpse.htm

Springer, Rebecca Ruter. Intra Muros, My Dream
of Heaven.
Old Tappen, New Jersey: Fleming H. Revell
Company, 1979.

Duplantis, Jesse. Heaven: Close Encounters of The
God Kind.
Tulsa, OK: Harrison House, 1996 P. 71, 103.
http://www.jdm.org/

Billy Graham Evangelistic Association
http://www.billygraham.org/Default.asp?bhcp=1

BriteBooks
http://www.britebooks.org

ONE LAST FAMILY PHOTO

YES... I know this is not a real Monkey, but I have not told Tommy. I don't want to break his heart. Let's keep it our little secret just between you and me.

Below is a completed example of the Headed For Heaven Certificates on the next 3 pages. This certificate is designed to help you and or your child recover from the loss of a pet or animal friend.

Start by thinking about the comforting evidence you read of pets and other animals in Heaven. Review Section Five: "How To Live With Your Pet Forever". Go over the prayer and then fill out the certificate stating that you believe and declare that your pet or animal friend is in Heaven now and you have decided to go to Heaven too.

If you need more than 3, BriteBooks has given you permission to copy the certificate for personal use only. By making a copy you can display it in a place easy to review when grief wants to overcome you or your child.

Example

By completing this certificate I do hereby declare that I believe my beloved

_____*Your pet or animal friend's name goes here*_____ has gone to Heaven and is waiting to be united with me once again.

I believe *Your pet or animal friend's name goes here*

is being well taken care of in Heaven, is happy and having a wonderful life.

I also declare that on the *The day 1st, 2nd etc.* day

of_____*Month name*_____ in the year _____*The year*_____ I have made the decision to receive God's Free Gift for me to go to Heaven too. Thank you Father God.

Because of the decision I made from this day forward I will no longer think of

_____*Your pet or animal friend's name goes here*_____

as just being in my past but now also in my future......

Certificate Of Declaration

Headed Toward Heaven

By completing this certificate I do hereby declare that I believe my beloved

_____

has gone to Heaven and is waiting to be united with me once again.

I believe_____
is being well taken care of in Heaven, is happy and having a wonderful life.

I also declare that on the _____ day

of_____ in the year _____
I have made the decision to receive God's Free Gift for me to go to Heaven too. Thank you Father God.

Because of the decision I made from this day forward I will no longer think of

_____

as just being in my past but now also in my future.

_____
Declared by: (Sign here)

_____
Witnessed by: (Sign here)

Certificate Of Declaration

Headed Toward Heaven

By completing this certificate I do hereby declare that I believe my beloved

_____

has gone to Heaven and is waiting to be united with me once again.

I believe_____
is being well taken care of in Heaven, is happy and having a wonderful life.

I also declare that on the _____ day

of_____ in the year _____
I have made the decision to receive God's Free Gift for me to go to Heaven too. Thank you Father God.

Because of the decision I made from this day forward I will no longer think of

_____

as just being in my past but now also in my future.

_____
Declared by: (Sign here)

_____
Witnessed by: (Sign here)

Headed Toward Heaven

By completing this certificate I do hereby declare that I believe my beloved

_____

has gone to Heaven and is waiting to be united with me once again.

I believe_____
is being well taken care of in Heaven, is happy and having a wonderful life.

I also declare that on the _____ day

of_____ in the year _____
I have made the decision to receive God's Free Gift for me to go to Heaven too. Thank you Father God.

Because of the decision I made from this day forward I will no longer think of

_____

as just being in my past but now also in my future.

_____
Declared by: (Sign here)

_____
Witnessed by: (Sign here)

JUST RELEASED "NEW"

Pets In Heaven Activity Book

This Activity Book is a comforting interactive tool to help you explain the difficult and emotional subject of a Pet's death to children.

Watch your child go from grief to <u>JOY</u> as they visualize their pet in Heaven

OVER 50 pages of fun activities that will <u>Comfort</u> your child!

Your child will have hours of fun as they do over 50 pages of activities..... Coloring pictures of pets in Heaven, Word search games, Crossword puzzles, Fun mazes and more.

This is the most unique and comforting children's Activity Book you will ever see -- Every Parent & Grandparent needs one as a tool to help their child recover from the grief of a pet's death.

-- Order Today --

$12.95 + $4 S/H (Michigan residents please add 6% tax)

For Credit Cards: order on-line at: **www.BriteBooks.org**
Or mail Check or Money Order to: BriteBooks, Dept. 71,
P.O. Box 801, Ortonville, MI 48462-0801.